T5-AQA-747

PAUL AS EXPERIENT

PAUL
AS EXPERIENT

By

Henry Burton Sharman Ph D

Honorary Lecturer in the Department of History
Yenching University Peking China

HARPER & BROTHERS PUBLISHERS
New York

PAUL AS EXPERIENT

Printed in the United States of America

I-X

First Impression 1945
Second Impression 1947
Third Impression 1948

LETTERS of Paul are revelatory not mainly of a body of concepts the product of intellection and reflection. Rather they are primarily the portrayal of the outcomes of an indubitable experience, itself based on an attitude taken by Paul which is disclosed by his exposition—though obscured, rather than illumined, by the frequent choice of one single Term wherewith to compass the content and quality of that creative attitude.

℧ Paul must regrettably remain an unsolvable psychological enigma, in his religious experience and in his subsequent reflection on that experience, to that explorer whose recourse is primarily to that single Term which is central with Paul. No single Term in language holds within itself the potentiality to express that which conditions the creation of that experience through which Paul went and which he subsequently set forth as available to others.

℧ Single terms are conveniences, may become expedients, possibly cannot be easily avoided in the advancement of a cause; but they are not fully adequate illuminants to cover the mode of the access of man to God.

℧ Paul was, subsequent to Jesus, the fashioner of what is probably regarded rightly as the most profound religious discovery in the quest of man for God. He was clearly and vividly conscious of that which conditioned his experience, whether or not it could be compassed adequately by any single Term.

℃ The most considerable element in the revelations made by Paul through his Letters is his vital and brilliantly intelligible disclosure of that basic attitude on the part of man which conditions the access of man to God and of God to man. That may be learned only by resolutely blotting out everywhere the term FAITH, and determinedly searching for the content of the creative conception covered by it in the extended expositions lodged here and there in the Letters of Paul.

℃ But that secret will naturally not be unveiled by customary cursory reading. Felt familiarity with the wording should be regarded as the most serious threat to an adequate understanding and sound evaluation. One must rather be keenly conscious steadily of the sole purpose of the exploration, namely, the discovery of what actually was, for the mind of Paul, that basic and creative attitude of the spirit of man upon which alone depends the accession of God to the life of man. That attitude Paul learned by experience, not by intellection. But the experience was itself the product of a profound process discoverable in the Letters of Paul—though not disclosed by any pondering of the term FAITH.

AN IDEAL OF PAUL

HOWBEIT in the church I had rather speak five
words with my understanding, that I might
instruct others also, than ten thousand
unintelligible words.

KING Agrippa said unto Paul, Thou art permitted to speak for thyself. Then Paul stretched forth his hand, and made his defence: I think myself happy, king Agrippa, that I am to make my defence before thee this day touching all the things whereof I am accused by the Jews: especially because thou art expert in all customs and questions which are among the Jews: wherefore I beseech thee to hear me patiently.

⁋ My manner of life then from my youth up, which was from the beginning among mine own nation, and at Jerusalem, know all the Jews; having knowledge of me from the first, if they be willing to testify, how that after the straitest sect of our religion I lived a Pharisee.

⁋ And now I stand here to be judged for the hope of the promise made of God unto our fathers; unto which promise our twelve tribes, earnestly serving God night and day, hope to attain. And concerning this hope I am accused by the Jews, O king! Why is it judged incredible with you, if God doth raise the dead?

⁋ I verily thought with myself, that I ought to do many things contrary to the name of Jesus of Nazareth. And this I also did in Jerusalem: and I both shut up many of the saints in prisons, having received authority from the chief priests, and when they were put to death, I gave my vote against them. And punishing them oftentimes in all the synagogues, I strove to make them blaspheme; and being exceedingly mad against them, I persecuted them even unto foreign cities.

℃ Whereupon as I journeyed to Damascus with the authority and commission of the chief priests, at midday, O king, I saw on the way a light from heaven, above the brightness of the sun, shining round about me and them that journeyed with me. And when we were all fallen to the earth, I heard a voice saying unto me in the Hebrew language, Saul, Saul, why persecutest thou me? it is hard for thee to kick against the goad. And I said, Who art thou, Lord? And the Lord said, I am Jesus whom thou persecutest.

℃ But arise, and stand upon thy feet: for to this end have I appeared unto thee, to appoint thee a minister and a witness both of the things wherein thou hast seen me, and of the things wherein I will appear unto thee; delivering thee from the people, and from the Gentiles, unto whom I send thee, to open their eyes, that they may turn from darkness to light, and from the power of Satan unto God, that they may receive remission of sins and an inheritance among them that are sanctified by faith in me.

BRETHREN, I make known to you, as touching the gospel which was preached by me, that it is not after man. For neither did I receive it from man, nor was I taught it, but it came to me through revelation of Jesus Christ.

℃ For ye have heard of my manner of life in time past in the Jews' religion, how that beyond measure I persecuted the church of God, and made havock of it: and I advanced in the Jews' religion beyond many of mine own age among my countrymen, being more exceedingly zealous for the traditions of my fathers.

℃ But when it was the good pleasure of God, who separated me, even from my mother's womb, and called me through his grace, to reveal his Son in me, that I might preach him among the Gentiles; immediately I conferred not with flesh and blood: neither went I up to Jerusalem to them which were apostles before me: but I went away into Arabia; and again I returned unto Damascus.

§3 PAUL AS EXPERIENT

KNOWING that a man is not justified by the
works of the Law, but only through Faith in
Jesus Christ, even we Jews believed on Christ
Jesus, that we might be justified by Faith in Christ,
and not by the works of the Law: because
by the works of the Law shall no flesh
be justified.

THROUGH the Law I died unto the Law, that I might live unto God. I have been crucified with Christ; yet I live; and yet no longer I, but Christ liveth in me: and that life which I now live in the flesh I live in Faith, the Faith which is in the Son of God, who loved me, and gave himself up for me. I do not make void the grace of God: for if righteousness is through the Law, then Christ died for nought.

℃ O foolish Galatians, who did bewitch you, before whose eyes Jesus Christ was openly set forth crucified? This only would I learn from you, Received ye the Spirit by the works of the Law, or by the hearing of Faith? Are ye so foolish? having begun in the Spirit, are ye now perfected in the flesh? Did ye suffer so many things in vain? if it be indeed in vain. He therefore that supplieth to you the Spirit, and worketh miracles among you, doeth he it by the works of the Law, or by the hearing of Faith?

§5 Paul As Experient

As many as are of the works of the Law are under a curse: for it is written, Cursed is every one which continueth not in all things that are written in the book of the Law, to do them. Now that no man is justified by the Law in the sight of God, is evident: for, The righteous shall live by Faith; and the Law is not of Faith; but, He that doeth them shall live in them. Christ redeemed us from the curse of the Law, having become a curse for us: for it is written, Cursed is every one that hangeth on a tree: that upon the Gentiles might come the blessing of Abraham in Christ Jesus; that we might receive the promise of the Spirit through Faith.

WHAT then is the Law? It was added because of transgressions, till the seed should come to whom the promise hath been made. Is the Law then against the promises of God? God forbid: for if there had been a law given which could make alive, verily righteousness would have been of the Law. Howbeit the scripture hath shut up all things under sin, that the promise by Faith in Jesus Christ might be given to them that believe.

℄ But before Faith came, we were kept in ward under the Law, shut up unto the faith which should afterwards be revealed. So that the Law hath been our tutor to bring us unto Christ, that we might be justified by Faith. But now that Faith is come, we are no longer under a tutor.

℄ For ye are all sons of God, through Faith, in Christ Jesus. For as many of you as were baptized into Christ did put on Christ. There can be neither Jew nor Greek, there can be neither bond nor free, there can be no male and female: for ye all are one in Christ Jesus.

So long as the heir is a child, he differeth nothing from a bondservant, though he is lord of all; but is under guardians and stewards until the term appointed of the father. So we also, when we were children, were held in bondage under the rudiments of the world.

℃ But when the fulness of the time came, God sent forth his Son, born of a woman, born under the Law, that he might redeem them which were under the Law, that we might receive the adoption of sons.

℃ And because ye are sons, God sent forth the Spirit of his Son into our hearts, crying, Abba, Father. So that thou art no longer a bond-servant, but a son; and if a son, then an heir through God.

§8 Paul As Experient

My little children, of whom I am again in travail until Christ be formed in you, yea, I
could wish to be present with you now, and to
change my voice; for I am perplexed about you.
℃ Tell me, ye that desire to be under the Law, do
ye not hear the Law?
℃ With freedom did Christ set us free: stand
fast therefore, and be not entangled again
in a yoke of bondage.

BEHOLD, I Paul say unto you, that, if ye receive circumcision, Christ will profit you nothing. Yea, I testify again to every man that receiveth circumcision, that he is a debtor to do the whole Law. Ye are severed from Christ, ye who would be justified by the Law; ye are fallen away from grace. For we through the Spirit by Faith wait for the hope of righteousness. For in Christ Jesus neither circumcision availeth anything, nor uncircumcision; but Faith working through love.

❧ For ye, brethren, were called for freedom; only use not your freedom for an occasion to the flesh, but through love be servants one to another. For the whole Law is fulfilled in one word, even in this; Thou shalt love thy neighbour as thyself.

WALK by the Spirit, and ye shall not fulfil the lust of the flesh. For the flesh lusteth against the Spirit, and the Spirit against the flesh; for these are contrary the one to the other; that ye may not do the things that ye would. But if ye are led by the Spirit, ye are not under the Law.

ℂ Now the works of the flesh are manifest, which are these, fornication, uncleanness, lasciviousness, idolatry, sorcery, enmities, strife, jealousies, wraths, factions, divisions, heresies, envyings, drunkenness, revellings, and such like: of the which I forewarn you, even as I did forewarn you, that they which practise such things shall not inherit the kingdom of God.

ℂ The fruit of the Spirit is love, joy, peace, long-suffering, kindness, goodness, faithfulness, meekness, temperance: against such there is no law.

ℂ And they that are of Christ Jesus have crucified the flesh with the passions and the lusts thereof. If we live by the Spirit, by the Spirit let us also walk.

ℂ Be not deceived; God is not mocked: for whatsoever a man soweth, that shall he also reap. For he that soweth unto his own flesh shall of the flesh reap corruption; but he that soweth unto the Spirit shall of the Spirit reap eternal life.

§11 Paul As Experient

FAR be it from me to glory, save in the cross of
our Lord Jesus Christ, through which the world
hath been crucified unto me, and I unto the world.
For neither is circumcision anything, nor uncircumcision, but a new creature.

JEWS ask for signs, and Greeks seek after wisdom:
but we preach Christ crucified, unto Jews a
stumblingblock, and unto Gentiles foolishness; but
unto them that are called, both Jews and Greeks,
Christ the power of God, and the wisdom of God.
℗ Of him are ye in Christ Jesus, who was made
unto us wisdom from God, and righteousness,
and sanctification, and redemption.

BRETHREN, when I came unto you, I came not with excellency of speech or of wisdom, proclaiming to you the mystery of God. For I determined not to know anything among you, save Jesus Christ, and him crucified. And I was with you in weakness, and in fear, and in much trembling. And my speech and my preaching were not in persuasive words of wisdom, but in demonstration of the Spirit and of power: that your Faith should not stand in the wisdom of men, but in the power of God.

UNTO us God revealed through the Spirit: for the Spirit searcheth all things, yea, the deep things of God. For who among men knoweth the things of a man, save the spirit of the man, which is in him? even so the things of God none knoweth, save the Spirit of God.

℃ But we received, not the spirit of the world, but the Spirit which is of God; that we might know the things that are freely given to us by God. Which things also we speak, not in words which man's wisdom teacheth, but which the Spirit teach-eth; comparing spiritual things with spiritual.

℃ Now the natural man receiveth not the things of the Spirit of God: for they are foolishness unto him; and he cannot know them, because they are spiritually judged. But he that is spiritual judgeth all things, and he himself is judged of no man. For who hath known the mind of the Lord, that he should instruct him? But we have the mind of Christ.

§15 PAUL AS EXPERIENT

ACCORDING to the grace of God which was given unto me, as a wise masterbuilder I laid a foundation; and another buildeth thereon. But let each man take heed how he buildeth thereon. For other foundation can no man lay than that which is laid, which is Jesus Christ.

§16 PAUL AS EXPERIENT

KNOW ye not that ye are a temple of God, and
that the Spirit of God dwelleth in you? If any
man destroyeth the temple of God, him shall God
destroy; for the temple of God is holy,
which temple ye are.

§17 Paul As Experient

For all things are yours; whether Paul, or Apollos, or Cephas, or the world, or life, or death, or things present, or things to come; all are yours; and ye are Christ's; and Christ is God's.

§18 Paul As Experient

Such were some of you: but ye were washed,
but ye were sanctified, but ye were justified in
the name of the Lord Jesus Christ, and in the
Spirit of our God.

KNOW ye not that your bodies are members of Christ? shall I then take away the members of Christ, and make them members of a harlot? God forbid. Or know ye not that he that is joined to a harlot is one body? for, The twain, saith he, shall become one flesh. But he that is joined unto the Lord is one spirit.

℃ Flee fornication. Every sin that a man doeth is without the body; but he that committeth fornication sinneth against his own body. Or know ye not that your body is a temple of the Holy Spirit which is in you, which ye have from God? and ye are not your own; for ye were bought with a price: glorify God therefore in your body.

§20 PAUL AS EXPERIENT

CIRCUMCISION is nothing, and uncircumcision is nothing; but the keeping of the commandments of God.

§21 Paul As Experient

H E that was called in the Lord, being a bond-servant, is the Lord's freedman: likewise he that was called, being free, is Christ's bondservant.

Though I was free from all men, I brought my-self under bondage to all, that I might gain the more. And to the Jews I became as a Jew, that I might gain Jews; to them that are under the Law, as under the Law, (not being myself under the Law,) that I might gain them that are under the Law; to them that are without law, as without law, (not being without law to God, but under law to Christ,) that I might gain them that are without law. To the weak I became weak, that I might gain the weak: I am become all things to all men, that I may by all means save some.

§23 PAUL AS EXPERIENT

No man speaking in the Spirit of God saith, Jesus is anathema; and no man can say, Jesus is Lord, but in the Holy Spirit.

IF I speak with the tongues of men and of angels, but have not love, I am become sounding brass, or a clanging cymbal. And if I have the gift of prophecy, and know all mysteries and all knowledge; and if I have all faith, so as to remove mountains, but have not love, I am nothing. And if I bestow all my goods to feed the poor, and if I give my body to be burned, but have not love, it profiteth me nothing.

℃ Love suffereth long, and is kind; love envieth not; love vaunteth not itself, is not puffed up, doth not behave itself unseemly, seeketh not its own, is not provoked, taketh not account of evil; rejoiceth not in unrighteousness, but rejoiceth with the truth; beareth all things, believeth all things, hopeth all things, endureth all things.

℃ Love never faileth: but whether there be prophecies, they shall be done away; whether there be tongues, they shall cease; whether there be knowledge, it shall be done away. For we know in part, and we prophesy in part: but when that which is perfect is come, that which is in part shall be done away.

℃ But now abideth faith, hope, love, these three; and the greatest of these is love.

BRETHREN, I make known unto you the gospel which I preached unto you, which also ye received, wherein also ye stand, by which also ye are saved; I make known, I say, in what words I preached it unto you, if ye hold it fast, except ye believed in vain.

℃ For I delivered unto you first of all that which also I received, how that Christ died for our sins according to the scriptures; and that he was buried; and that he hath been raised on the third day according to the scriptures.

℃ And that he appeared to Cephas; then to the twelve; then he appeared to about five hundred brethren at once, of whom the greater part remain until now, but some are fallen asleep; then he appeared to James; then to all the apostles; and last of all, as unto one born out of due time, he appeared to me also.

℃ For I am the least of the apostles, that am not meet to be called an apostle, because I persecuted the church of God. But by the grace of God I am what I am: and his grace which was bestowed upon me was not found vain; but I laboured more abundantly than they all: yet not I, but the grace of God which was with me.

SINCE by man came death, by man came also the resurrection of the dead. For as in Adam all die, so also in Christ shall all be made alive.

℃ The first man Adam became a living soul. The last Adam became a life-giving spirit.

℃ Death is swallowed up in victory. O death, where is thy victory? O death, where is thy sting? The sting of death is sin; and the power of sin is the Law: but thanks be to God, which giveth us the victory through our Lord Jesus Christ.

§27 PAUL AS EXPERIENT

Now he that stablisheth us with you in Christ,
and anointed us, is God; who also sealed us,
and gave us the earnest of the Spirit
in our hearts.

ARE we beginning again to commend ourselves? or need we, as do some, epistles of commendation to you or from you? Ye are our epistle, written in our hearts, known and read of all men; being made manifest that ye are an epistle of Christ, ministered by us, written not with ink, but with the Spirit of the living God; not in tables of stone, but in tables that are hearts of flesh.

℃ God made us ministers of a new covenant; not of the letter, but of the spirit: for the letter killeth, but the Spirit giveth Life.

℃ If the ministration of death, written, and engraven on stones, came with glory, so that the children of Israel could not look stedfastly upon the face of Moses for the glory of his face; which glory was passing away: how shall not rather the ministration of the Spirit be with glory? For if the ministration of condemnation is glory, much rather doth the ministration of righteousness exceed in glory. For if that which passeth away was with glory, much more that which remaineth is in glory.

§29 Paul As Experient

Now the Lord is the Spirit: and where the Spirit of the Lord is, there is liberty. But we all, with unveiled face reflecting as a mirror the glory of the Lord, are transformed into the same image from glory to glory, even as from the Lord the Spirit.

§30 Paul As Experient

ALWAYS bearing about in the body the dying of Jesus, that the life also of Jesus may be manifested in our body. For we which live are alway delivered unto death for Jesus' sake, that the life also of Jesus may be manifested in our mortal flesh.

§31 Paul As Experient

THE love of Christ constraineth us; because we thus judge, that one died for all, therefore all died; and he died for all, that they which live should no longer live unto themselves, but unto him who for their sakes died and rose again.
¶ Wherefore if any man is in Christ, he is a new creature: the old things are passed away; behold, they are become new.

In everything commending ourselves, as ministers of God, in much patience, in afflictions, in necessities, in distresses, in stripes, in imprisonment, in tumults, in labours, in watchings, in fastings; in pureness, in knowledge, in longsuffering, in kindness, in the Holy Spirit, in love unfeigned, in the word of truth, in the power of God.

℃ By the armour of righteousness on the right hand and on the left, by glory and dishonour, by evil report and good report.

℃ As deceivers, and yet true; as unknown, and yet well known; as dying, and behold, we live; as chastened, and not killed; as sorrowful, yet alway rejoicing; as poor, yet making many rich; as having nothing, and yet possessing all things.

§33 Paul As Experient

For ye know the grace of our Lord Jesus Christ,
that, though he was rich, yet for your sakes
he became poor, that ye through his
poverty might become rich.

§34 Paul As Experient

BRINGING every thought into captivity to the obedience of Christ.

§35 PAUL AS EXPERIENT

His letters, they say, are weighty and strong; but his bodily presence is weak, and his speech of no account.

But I fear, lest by any means, as the serpent beguiled Eve in his craftiness, your minds should be corrupted from the simplicity and the purity that is toward Christ. For if he that cometh preacheth another Jesus, whom we did not preach, or if ye receive a different Spirit, which ye did not receive, or a different gospel, which ye did not accept, ye do well to bear with him!

WHEREINSOEVER any is bold (I speak in foolishness), I am bold also. Are they Hebrews? so am I. Are they Israelites? so am I. Are they the seed of Abraham? so am I. Are they ministers of Christ? (I speak as one beside himself) I more; in labours more abundantly, in prisons more abundantly, in stripes above measure, in deaths oft.

℄ Of the Jews five times received I forty stripes save one. Thrice was I beaten with rods, once was I stoned, thrice I suffered shipwreck, a night and a day have I been in the deep.

℄ In journeyings often, in perils of rivers, in perils of robbers, in perils from my countrymen, in perils from the Gentiles, in perils in the city, in perils in the wilderness, in perils in the sea, in perils among false brethren; in labour and travail, in watchings often, in hunger and thirst, in fastings often, in cold and nakedness.

℄ Beside those things that are without, there is that which presseth upon me daily, anxiety for all the churches. Who is weak, and I am not weak? who is made to stumble, and I burn not? If I must needs glory, I will glory of the things that concern my weakness.

THOUGH it is not expedient, I must needs glory:
but I will come to visions and revelations of
the Lord. I know a man in Christ, fourteen years
ago (whether in the body, I know not; or whether
out of the body, I know not; God knoweth), such
a one caught up even to the third heaven. And I
know such a man (whether in the body, or apart
from the body, I know not; God knoweth), how
that he was caught up into Paradise, and heard
unspeakable words, which it is not lawful for a
man to utter.

⁋ On behalf of such a one will I glory: but on
mine own behalf I will not glory, save in my
weaknesses. For if I should desire to glory, I shall
not be foolish; for I shall speak the truth: but I forbear, lest any man should account of me above
that which he seeth me to be, or heareth from me.
⁋ And by reason of the exceeding greatness of
the revelations—wherefore, that I should not be
exalteth overmuch, there was given to me a thorn

in the flesh, a messenger of Satan to buffet me,
that I should not be exalteth overmuch. Concerning this thing I besought the Lord thrice, that it
might depart from me. And he hath said unto me,
My grace is sufficient for thee: for my power is
made perfect in weakness. Most gladly therefore
will I rather glory in my weaknesses, that the
power of Christ may rest upon me. Wherefore
I take pleasure in weaknesses, in injuries, in necessities, in persecutions, in distresses, for
Christ's sake: for when I am weak, then
am I strong.

§39 Paul As Experient

Know ye not as to your own selves, that Jesus
Christ is in you? unless indeed ye
be reprobate.

For I am not ashamed of the gospel: for it is
the power of God unto salvation to every one
that believeth; to the Jew first, and also to the
Greek. For therein is revealed a righteousness of
God by Faith unto faith: as it is written,
But the righteous shall live
by Faith.

THERE is no respect of persons with God. For as many as have sinned without law shall also perish without law: and as many as have sinned under Law shall be judged by Law; for not the hearers of a Law are just before God, but the doers of a Law shall be justified: for when Gentiles which have no law do by nature the things of the Law, these, having no law, are a law unto themselves; in that they shew the work of the Law written in their hearts, their conscience bearing witness therewith, and their thoughts one with another accusing or else excusing them.

CIRCUMCISION indeed profiteth, if thou be a doer of the Law: but if thou be a transgressor of the Law, thy circumcision is become uncircumcision. If therefore the uncircumcision keep the ordinances of the Law, shall not his uncircumcision be reckoned for circumcision? and shall not the uncircumcision which is by nature, if it fulfil the Law, judge thee, who with the letter and circumcision art a transgressor of the Law?

℄ For he is not a Jew, which is one outwardly; neither is that circumcision, which is outward in the flesh: but he is a Jew, which is one inwardly; and circumcision is that of the heart, in the spirit, not in the letter.

WHAT advantage hath the Jew? or what is the
profit of circumcision? Much every way:
first of all, that they were intrusted with the
oracles of God. For what if some were without
Faith? shall their want of Faith make of none
effect the faithfulness of God?
God forbid.

By the works of the Law shall no flesh be justified in the sight of God: for through the Law cometh the knowledge of sin. But now apart from the Law a righteousness of God hath been manifested, being witnessed by the law and the prophets; even the righteousness of God through Faith in Jesus Christ unto all them that believe. For there is no distinction; for all have sinned, and fall short of the glory of God; being justified freely by his grace through the redemption that is in Christ Jesus.

Where is the glorying? It is excluded. By what manner of law? of Works? Nay: but by a law of Faith. We reckon therefore that a man is justified by Faith apart from the works of the Law. Or is God the God of Jews only? is he not the God of Gentiles also? Yea, of Gentiles also, if so be that God is one: and he shall justify the circumcision by Faith, and the uncircumcision through Faith. Do we then make the Law of none effect through Faith? God forbid: nay, we establish the Law.

§46 PAUL AS EXPERIENT

FAITH was reckoned unto Abraham for right-eousness. Now it was not written for his sake alone, that it was reckoned unto him; but for our sake also, unto whom it shall be reckoned, who believe on him that raised Jesus our Lord from the dead, who was delivered up for our trespasses, and was raised for
our justification.

§47 Paul As Experient

THE love of God hath been shed abroad in our
hearts through the Holy Spirit which
was given unto us.

WHILE we were yet weak, in due season Christ died for the ungodly. For scarcely for a righteous man will one die: for peradventure for the good man some one would even dare to die. But God commendeth his own love toward us, in that, while we were yet sinners, Christ died for us.

℄ If, while we were enemies, we were reconciled to God through the death of his Son, much more, being reconciled, shall we be saved by his life.

THROUGH one man sin entered into the world, and death through sin; and so death passed unto all men, for that all sinned:—for until the Law sin was in the world: but sin is not imputed when there is no Law. Nevertheless death reigned from Adam until Moses, even over them that had not sinned after the likeness of Adam's transgression, who is a figure of him that was to come.
℄ But not as the trespass, so also is the free gift. For if by the trespass of the one the many died, much more did the grace of God, and the gift by the grace of the one man, Jesus Christ, abound unto the many. And not as through one that sinned, so is the gift: for the judgement came of one unto condemnation, but the free gift came of many trespasses unto justification.
℄ For if, by the trespass of the one, death reigned through the one; much more shall they that receive the abundance of grace and of the gift of righteousness reign in life through the one, even Jesus Christ.
℄ So then as through one trespass the judgement came unto all men to condemnation; even so

through one act of righteousness the free gift came
unto all men to justification of life. For as through
the one man's disobedience the many were made
sinners, even so through the obedience of the one
shall the many be made righteous.

℃ And the Law came in beside, that the trespass
might abound; but where sin abounded, grace did
abound more exceedingly: that, as sin reigned in
death, even so might grace reign through
righteousness unto eternal life through
Jesus Christ our Lord.

WHAT shall we say? Shall we continue in sin, that grace may abound? God forbid. We who died to sin, how shall we any longer live therein? Or are ye ignorant that all we who were baptized into Christ Jesus were baptized into his death? We were buried therefore with him through baptism into death: that like as Christ was raised from the dead through the glory of the Father, so we also might walk in newness of life. ⁋ For if we have become united with him by the likeness of his death, we shall be also by the likeness of his resurrection; knowing this, that our old man was crucified with him, that the body of sin might be done away, that so we should no longer be in bondage to sin; for he that hath died is justified from sin.

⁋ But if we died with Christ, we believe that we shall also live with him; knowing that Christ being raised from the dead dieth no more; death no more hath dominion over him. For the death that he died, he died unto sin once: but the life that he liveth, he liveth unto God. Even so reckon ye also yourselves to be dead unto sin, but alive unto God in Christ Jesus.

§51 Paul As Experient

LET not sin reign in your mortal body, that ye should obey the lusts thereof: neither present your members unto sin as instruments of unrighteousness; but present yourselves unto God, as alive from the dead, and your members as instruments of righteousness unto God. For sin shall not have dominion over you: for ye are not under Law, but under grace.

KNOW ye not, that to whom ye present yourselves as servants unto obedience, his servants ye are whom ye obey; whether of sin unto death, or of obedience unto righteousness? But thanks be to God, that, whereas ye were servants of sin, ye became obedient from the heart to that form of teaching whereunto ye were delivered; and being made free from sin, ye became servants of righteousness.

℃ I speak after the manner of men because of the infirmity of your flesh: for as ye presented your members as servants to uncleanness and to iniquity unto iniquity, even so now present your members as servants to righteousness unto sanctification.

℃ For when ye were servants of sin, ye were free in regard of righteousness. What fruit then had ye at that time in the things whereof ye are now ashamed? for the end of those things is death. But now being made free from sin, and become servants to God, ye have your fruit unto sanctification, and the end eternal life. For the wages of sin is death; but the free gift of God is eternal life in Christ Jesus our Lord.

WHEREFORE, my brethren, ye also were made dead to the Law through the body of Christ; that ye should be joined to another, even to him who was raised from the dead, that we might bring forth fruit unto God. For when we were in the flesh, the sinful passions, which were through the Law, wrought in our members to bring forth fruit unto death. But now we have been discharged from the Law, having died to that wherein we were holden; so that we serve in newness of the Spirit, and not in oldness of the Letter.

THE Law is holy, and the commandment holy, and righteous, and good. Did then that which is good become death unto me? God forbid. But sin, that it might be shewn to be sin, by working death to me through that which is good;—that through the commandment sin might become exceeding sinful. For we know that the Law is spiritual: but I am carnal, sold under sin.

℧ For that which I do I know not: for not what I would, that do I practise; but what I hate, that I do. But if what I would not, that I do, I consent unto the Law that it is good. So now it is no more I that do it, but Sin which dwelleth in me. For I know that in me, that is, in my flesh, dwelleth no good thing: for to will is present with me, but to do that which is good is not. For the good which I would I do not: but the evil which I would not, that I practise. But if what I would not, that I do, it is no more I that do it, but Sin which dwelleth in me.

℧ I find then the law, that, to me who would do good, evil is present. For I delight in the Law of

God after the inward man: but I see a different
law in my members, warring against the law of
my mind, and bringing me into captivity under
the law of sin which is in my members.

℃ O wretched man that I am! who shall deliver
me out of the body of this death? I thank
God through Jesus Christ
our Lord.

THERE is no condemnation to them that are in Christ Jesus. For the Law of the Spirit of Life in Christ Jesus made me free from the law of sin and of death. For what the Law could not do, in that it was weak through the flesh, God, sending his own Son in the likeness of sinful flesh and for sin, condemned sin in the flesh: that the ordinance of the Law might be fulfilled in us, who walk not after the Flesh, but after the Spirit.

℀ For they that are after the flesh do mind the things of the flesh; but they that are after the spirit the things of the spirit. For the mind of the flesh is Death; but the mind of the spirit is Life and peace: because the mind of the flesh is enmity against God; for it is not subject to the law of God, neither indeed can it be: and they that are in the flesh cannot please God. But ye are not in the Flesh, but in the Spirit, if so be that the Spirit of God dwelleth in you.

℀ But if any man hath not the Spirit of Christ, he is none of his. And if Christ is in you, the body is dead because of sin; but the spirit is life because of righteousness. But if the Spirit of him that raised up Jesus from the dead dwelleth in you, he that raised up Christ Jesus from the dead shall quicken also your mortal bodies through his Spirit that dwelleth in you.

℃ So then, brethren, we are debtors, not to the flesh, to live after the flesh: for if ye live after the flesh, ye must die; but if by the Spirit ye mortify the deeds of the body, ye shall live. For as many as are led by the Spirit of God, these are sons of God. For ye received not the spirit of bondage again unto fear; but ye received the spirit of adoption, whereby we cry, Abba, Father. The Spirit himself beareth witness with our spirit, that we are children of God: and if children, then heirs; heirs of God, and joint-heirs with Christ.

§56 Paul As Experient

CONFORMED to the image of his Son, that he might be the firstborn among many brethren.

BRETHREN, by the mercies of God, I beseech
you to present your bodies a living sacrifice,
holy, acceptable to God, which is your reasonable
service. And be not fashioned according to this
world: but be ye transformed by the renewing of
your mind, that ye may prove what is the
good and acceptable and perfect
will of God.

§58 Paul As Experient

E VEN as we have many members in one body,
and all the members have not the same office:
so we, who are many, are one body in Christ,
and severally members one of another.

OWE no man anything, save to love one another: for he that loveth his neighbour hath fulfilled the Law. For this, Thou shalt not commit adultery, Thou shalt not kill, Thou shalt not steal, Thou shalt not covet, and if there be any other commandment, it is summed up in this word, namely, Thou shalt love thy neighbour as thyself. Love worketh no ill to his neighbour: love therefore is the fulfilment of the Law.

§60 Paul As Experient

Have this mind in you, which was also in Christ Jesus: who, being in the form of God, counted it not a prize to be on an equality with God, but emptied himself, taking the form of a servant, being made in the likeness of men; and being found in fashion as a man, he humbled himself, becoming obedient even unto death, yea, the death of the cross. Wherefore also God highly exalted him, and gave unto him the name which is above every name.

HAVE no confidence in the flesh: though I my-self might have confidence even in the flesh: if any other man thinketh to have confidence in the flesh, I yet more: circumcised the eighth day, of the stock of Israel, of the tribe of Benjamin, a Hebrew of Hebrews; as touching the Law, a Pharisee; as touching zeal, persecuting the church; as touching the righteousness which is in the Law, found blameless.

WHAT things were gain to me, these have I counted loss for Christ. Yea verily, and I count all things to be loss for the excellency of the knowledge of Christ Jesus my Lord: for whom I suffered the loss of all things, and do count them but refuse, that I may gain Christ, and be found in him, not having a righteousness of mine own, even that which is of the Law, but that which is through Faith in Christ, the righteousness which is of God by Faith.

℣ That I may know him, and the power of his resurrection, and the fellowship of his sufferings, becoming conformed unto his death; if by any means I may attain unto the resurrection from the dead.

℣ Not that I have already obtained, or am already made perfect: but I press on, if so be that I may apprehend that for which also I was apprehended by Christ Jesus. Brethren, I count not myself yet to have apprehended: but one thing I do, forgetting the things which are behind, and stretching forward to the things which are before, I press on toward the goal unto the prize of the high calling of God in Christ Jesus.

In Christ ye were circumcised with a circumcision not made with hands, in the putting off
of the body of the flesh, in the circumcision of
Christ; having been buried with him in baptism,
wherein ye were also raised with him through
Faith in the working of God, who raised him from
the dead.

℃ And you, being dead through your trespasses
and the uncircumcision of your flesh, you, I say,
did he quicken together with him, having forgiven
us all our trespasses; having blotted out the bond
written in ordinances that was against us, which
was contrary to us: and he hath taken it out
of the way, nailing it to the cross.

§64 Paul As Experient

Ye died, and your life is hid with Christ in God.

Y E have put off the old man with his doings, and have put on the new man, which is being renewed unto knowledge after the image of him that created him: where there cannot be Greek and Jew, circumcision and uncircumcision, barbarian, Scythian, bondman, freeman: but Christ is all, and in all.

STUDIES IN
PAUL AS EXPERIENT

STUDIES IN PAUL
AS EXPERIENT

By

Henry Burton Sharman Ph D

Honorary Lecturer in the Department of History
Yenching University Peking China

HARPER & BROTHERS PUBLISHERS
New York

❧ "The hope of the promise made of God unto our fathers" : to what Jewish national hope does it seem probable Paul here made reference?

❧ "Why is it judged incredible with you, if God doth raise the dead?" : after how many centuries, in the passage of time, has such an event become credible to the mind of man?

❧ "Many things contrary to the name of Jesus of Nazareth" : contemplation of the deeds Paul thought he ought to do, and without hesitation or scruple violently did, discloses what psychic state favorable to radical upheaval?

❧ "Saul, Saul, why persecutest thou me? it is hard for thee to kick against the goad" : What precisely was the goad against which Paul had been kicking? Was it just broadly against Jesus? Was it against the annulment of the Law by Jesus? Was it against the reported claim by Jesus that he was the Christ? Was it against the exacting and absolute conditions set forth by Jesus as essential for acceptance by God? Was it against something that Jesus had taught must be believed before one could be accounted righteous? Or was the goad—what? If one cannot soundly surmise what the goad was, what is the prospect for an understanding of the experience of Paul?

⟪ "That they may turn from darkness to light" : what estimate should one place on this definition of the values to be had through the mediation of the religion of Jesus?

⟪ "Sanctified by faith in me" : what is the precise content of that faith in Jesus which is assuredly productive of sanctification?

℆ "It came to me through revelation of Jesus Christ" : judging from the account given, what form did that revelation take? Did it consist in spoken words chosen to convey concepts? Was it in the form of declarations as to how the events in the career of Jesus should be interpreted? Did its value consist solely in its demonstration that Jesus had been resurrected and was living? Who interpreted the significance of that asserted demonstration—Jesus to Paul? or Paul to mankind?

℆ "To reveal his Son in me" : that was the occasion when the sole corrective declaration to Paul was that it was hard for him to kick against the goad : When did he stop kicking? Why did he stop kicking? By the use of what element or elements in his nature did he stop kicking? Why did his stopping of his kicking result in that inward transformation by which he became what he subsequently called a new creature or creation?

⟨ "Justified" . . . "justified" . . . "justified" : what body of various alternative phrases might be offered as embodying adequately and lucidly the concept covered by this central term of Paul—"justified"?

⟨ "Faith in Jesus Christ" . . . "belief on Christ Jesus" : since the term "Faith" is of itself altogether ambiguous, the alternative offered here seems to demand exploration : "Belief" means believe what about Christ Jesus?

⟨ If it be supposed tentatively that "belief on Christ Jesus" means belief that Christ Jesus was God incarnate raised from the dead, what relation does that belief bear to human conduct?

⟨ What stage intervenes between believing something about Christ Jesus and doing something about righteousness?

℘ Where must the ethical norm and loyalty of what is called Faith rest if, because of its impotence, Law as norm is declared to be futile? What then may be regarded as a mode of designation more adequate and lucid than either Belief or Faith?

❡ "Died unto the Law" : an attitude taken by Paul in order that he might exercise that which superseded the Law, namely, what he elsewhere and here calls "Faith"?

❡ "That I might live unto God" : wherein essentially and basically consists the difference between living unto the Law and living unto God?

❡ "I have been crucified with Christ" : the last and most stubbornly held outpost of personality resides in what function of the human personality?

❡ "Christ liveth in me" : and was operative within Paul consciously in what significant dual capacity?

❡ "If righteousness is through the Law" : but if one has "died unto the Law" as the effective way to righteousness, the alternative to which Paul gave himself, according to his own assertion, was "that he might live unto God" : how bring this into intelligible harmony with the concept that the alternative was something achieved by the death of Christ?

℄ "This only would I learn from you" : what estimate should properly be placed upon that test to which Paul here makes his sole and determinative appeal?

℄ "Received ye the Spirit" : in what measure is this concept of a profound inner experience as the resultant of an adequate religious attitude an essential element of that Judaism within which Paul was reared? Whence did Paul derive his marked conviction that this experience was the most valid norm by which to determine the vitality of any religious Way?

℄ Paul employs this impressive norm in the fundamental contest between Law and Faith : what degree of validity has that norm, taken as the mode of determining the soundness or otherwise of contemporary theological doctrines within Christianity about the Way unto Life?

❡ "The Law is not of Faith; but, He that doeth them shall live in them" : when one abandons the Law as the Way of Life, and substitutes for it Faith as the Way, whence does one draw the controlling norms for conduct? By what process does Faith assure that the life will actually conform to these norms? Or is Faith to be regarded as the mode of being assured against the penalties which are inherent in non-conformity to these norms?

❡ "That we might receive the promise of the Spirit through Faith" : what actual practical benefit derives from the possession of the Spirit? What is the justification for regarding possession by the Spirit of God as worthy of being characterized as a Blessing?

❡ Why is it that the Spirit comes through Faith but does not come through Law?

⟪ In the contrast between Law and Faith, what was for Paul the determinative norm by which the validity of one as against the other was settled?

⟪ In what sense, or through what factors or out-comes in the pursuance of Law, should Law be considered a Tutor unto somebody or something other than Law?

⟪ "Ye are all sons of God" : wherein then consists any distinctiveness of Jesus?

⟪ "Did put on Christ" : by what method? What does the proposed method mean?

⟪ "Ye all are one" : wherein essentially does the unity consist, that is, what is the creative factor that accounts for the sense, and the validity of the sense, of unity?

❡ "That he might redeem them which were under the Law" : judging from the context parallel, the term "redeem," the concept of redemption, means from what status to what status?

❡ "God sent forth the Spirit of his Son into our hearts" : whether did that coming of the Spirit precede or follow the fulfilment of the condition for the attainment of the status? What was that condition, stated in clearly comprehensible terms?

❡ "So that thou art no longer a bondservant" : and therefore art free from obedience? or art free to obey what or whom?

℘ "Until Christ be formed in you" : whether is the deep solicitude of Paul here concerned with (1) correct belief, or (2) sound ethical action, or (3) basic reconstitution of personality, or (4) what?

℘ "With freedom did Christ set us free" : free to act after what manner? free to act after what, if any, restraint? free to make what, if any, choice? free to remain under the bondage of impulse or habit, or free to be free?

℘ "Be not entangled again in a yoke of bondage" : it being granted that one is able to choose whether or not to accept the bondage of a code, wherein consists, for Paul, the highway to release from the bondage of the flesh?

❡ "If ye receive circumcision, Christ will profit you nothing" : accepting the Pauline position as to the invalidity of an ancient Jewish rite, the Christian tends to substitute for it what rites that are regarded as modes of making Christ efficacious as a source of religious profit?

❡ "In Christ Jesus neither circumcision availeth anything, nor uncircumcision; but Faith working through love" : with what degree of accuracy, or otherwise, may it be affirmed, as a deduction from this assertion, that no religious rites actually avail anything, but only Faith working through love?

❡ "Use not your freedom for an occasion to the flesh" : if Law is abolished in favor of Faith, wherein is based the constraint that would inhibit the freedom of the flesh?

❡ "The whole Law is fulfilled in one word, even in this; Thou shalt love thy neighbour as thyself" : in what degree does that seem to read like the abolition of the Law in favor of Faith? It may be regarded as the abolition of what in favor of what? Wherein does it fall short, if at all, of being true religion?

℃ What is it that Paul says, in this passage, works through love? What does his chosen term mean? In what degree, and after what manner, does his chosen term introduce that which may properly be regarded as religious?

¶ "They that are of Christ Jesus have crucified the flesh with the passions and the lusts thereof" : since the basic problem is to overcome the fact that "ye may not do the things that ye would," that is, to overcome the impotence of the will when directed toward the conquest of specific passions and lusts, toward what or whom, or against whom or what, must the volitional thrust be directed if the step taken can adequately be covered only by the figure of crucifixion?

¶ "If ye are led by the Spirit, ye are not under the Law" : if not under the Law, then under what direction? And by what process or act or attitude does the individual come under that different direction?

℘ "The world hath been crucified unto me, and I unto the world" : if one should be profoundly impressed by the vigor and the reach of this portrayal of self-immolation, and should aspire to fellowship with Paul through its personal achievement, with the fulfilment of what condition is one confronted?

℘ "Neither is circumcision anything, nor uncircumcision, but a new creature" : judging by the position here taken by Paul, the function of an adequate and sound religion is nothing less than what? In view of the standard for outcome set by Paul, the means for its effective realization must of necessity have what character?

℃ "Christ the power of God, and the wisdom of God" : apparently for Paul not power manifested in "signs" for Jews; apparently for Paul not wisdom made evident through the skilled fashioning of an intellectual philosophy for Greeks: wherein then consisted the evidences of the power? the wisdom then had to do with illumination upon what basic problem?

℃ "Righteousness, and sanctification, and redemption" : highly pregnant terms surely! What does each one of them really mean?

§13 Studies in Paul as Experient

℄ "Not with excellency of speech or of wisdom" : "not in persuasive words of wisdom" : "not in the wisdom of men" : that which Paul would negative, as not standing within his province, had contemporary prevalence at the hands of what influence?

℄ "In demonstration of the Spirit and of power" : "in the power of God" : this power of God, this Spirit of God, demonstrated itself, through the medium of Paul, by the effecting of what convincing results or outcomes within the hearers who rightly understood and responded to the message?

℄ "That your Faith should not stand in the wisdom of men, but in the power of God" : in what degree is a Faith so based assailable?

ℂ "We received, not the spirit of the world, but the Spirit which is of God" : "We speak, not in words which man's wisdom teacheth, but which the Spirit teacheth" : "We have the mind of Christ" : for the possession and exercise of an accession to the human personality so significant and supreme, what basic condition obviously exists in the nature of the case and must be fulfilled?

❡ "Other foundation can no man lay than that which is laid, which is Jesus Christ" : on the basis of an unquestioning acceptance of the position here taken by Paul, where shall one go for the elements which should properly enter into the fashioning of the foundation, and provide the materials for building the superstructure upon it?

❡ As a foundation for a worthy religion, should appeal be made (1) to the episodes of a career and its end, or (2) to the concepts, and ideals, and insights which found expression through teaching, or (3) to the broad underlying manner of the personal life, or (4) to the revelation in words of basic life principle and its incarnation in deeds without relevance to their cost to the doer or whatever their cost to the doer, or (5) should appeal be made to—What, or to—Whom?

❦ "The Spirit of God dwelleth in you" : since this seems not to be an affirmation of Paul about man as man, but rather about the person who has fulfilled the condition for the accession of God to the life, the one who "destroyeth the temple of God" must obviously not be some external killer, but rather what eminent internal foe or foes?

❦ "Ye are a temple of God" : as against what concepts that are seemingly adequate to cover simply man as man?

❦ "The temple of God is holy" : so that for acceptable and observable objects of worship one may legitimately begin with the manifestation of God in richly regenerated human personality?

⫶ "Christ is God's" :how restate that position, in such form that it is not simply an affirmation, but rather becomes an intelligible and wholly justifiable statement of observable historical fact?

⫶ "Ye are Christ's" : if the sense in which that is true bears any recognizable analogy to the possession of Christ by God, then one does not become the possession of Christ until one has completely fulfilled what basic condition?

⫶ "All things are yours" : what relation does that as an assured and reasonable outcome bear to the definition of that which must be done as the mode to the achievement of that outcome?

❡ "In the name of the Lord Jesus Christ, and in the Spirit of our God" : such outcomes as are covered by the associated terms "washed," and "sanctified," and "justified" are in their nature so truly stupendous that clear knowledge of the effective means becomes imperative: whether was that means "the name of the Lord Jesus Christ" or rather "the Spirit of our God"? And if the latter, whereby and wherein did the Lord Jesus Christ make his contribution to the outcome?

❡ "Know ye not that your bodies are members of Christ?" : the body attains to that status by virtue of its being the seat of what within that can effect such an intimate union?

❡ "He that is joined unto the Lord is one spirit" : by what process specifically, and by what process alone, may that be wrought within an individual which makes that individual truly of one spirit with another individual?

❡ "Know ye not that your body is a temple of the Holy Spirit which is in you, which ye have from God" : bestowed by God upon whatever individual has fulfilled what basic and essential condition upon which that bestowal is wholly dependent?

❡ "Ye are not your own" : practically and specifically, how can any individual abdicate from self-possession to actual possession by another?

❡ "Circumcision is nothing, and uncircumcision is nothing; but the keeping of the commandments of God" : since it is the position of Paul that exercise of Faith has displaced the Law which expressed the commandments of God, what is the resource of one who would know what Paul meant by the commandments of God?

❡ "Circumcision is nothing, and uncircumcision is nothing; but"—What does matter? Since the outstanding answer of Paul in his letters is most often one word, namely, Faith, what measure of validity or otherwise would rest in the suggestion that Faith meant for Paul what he here states, namely, "the keeping of the commandments of God"? Wherein does that differ from keeping the Law? And apart from the Law, how can men know, according to Paul, what God desires done?

℃ "He that was called in the Lord, being a bond-servant, is the Lord's freedman" : slavery consists, ultimately, in having another human being as external master and director of the life: freedom consists, in the last analysis, in having as internal master and ultimate director of the essential life, What or Whom?

℃ "He that was called, being free, is Christ's bondservant" : on what basis or understanding can it be maintained that the free man has not actually lost fundamentally rather than gained through complete allegiance to Christ?

℄ "Not being myself under the Law" : that which Paul repeatedly and insistently set over against the Law, as that under which he lived and urged others to adopt, regarded as the means of acceptance with God and the guarantee of the gift of the Spirit of God, was covered by Paul through what single term?

℄ "Not being without law to God, but under law to Christ" : as a man who found the Law to be nothing better than impotent bondage, that to which actually he resorted as a way to declared potent freedom constitutes a secret worthy of the most luminous revelation possible by Paul. In what measure is that revelation achieved by this declaration "not being without law, but under law"?

℄ Precisely and lucidly, what does it mean to be under law to Christ or to God? Wherein essentially does that differ from being under some Code?

℃ "Jesus is anathema" . . . "Jesus is Lord" : these represent the extremes of evaluation: what is the source of those declarations of estimate which stand at neither extreme but somewhere or other between?

℃ "No man can say, Jesus is Lord, but in the Holy Spirit" : since the acquisition of the Holy Spirit is dependent upon what Paul calls, in summary, "Faith," the ultimately worthy estimate of Jesus follows upon, rather than precedes, the attitude covered by "Faith" : how define or describe that attitude as to make intelligible why that attitude produces inevitably and justifiably that resultant estimate of Jesus?

℄ "But now abideth faith, hope, love, these three; and the greatest of these is love" : wherein is the justification for regarding love as greater than even Faith itself?

℄ If one were to set "these three" down in what should be considered their natural chronological sequence, what would stand first and which would come last?

℄ In what degree is it practicable to command love? Whether is love a method or a product?

℄ Granted the superlative quality of love as conceived and envisioned by Paul, wherein consists its genesis within persons who may aspire to its possession and exercise?

℄ "That which also I received" : received by Paul from what source or sources?

℄ "How that Christ died for our sins according to the scriptures" : where within the Old Testament scriptures is it foretold that the Christ must die, and that on behalf of the sins of mankind?

℄ "How that Christ died for our sins according to the scriptures" : where within the Letters of Paul may one find citations from the Old Testament in support of the conviction that Christ died for our sins?

℄ "That Christ hath been raised on the third day according to the scriptures" : where within the Old Testament may one find passages which foretell that the Christ was destined to be raised from the dead?

℄ "That Christ hath been raised on the third day according to the scriptures" : at what points within the Letters of Paul may one discover citations from the Old Testament in support of the conviction that Christ was destined to be raised from the dead?

❡ "Since by man came death, by man came also the resurrection of the dead. For as in Adam all die, so also in Christ shall all be made alive" : according to the account in the Book of Genesis, the offence of Adam productive of Death for man may be covered completely by what single word? What legitimate deduction may be drawn therefrom as to that quality in Christ which produced Life in him and makes him productive of Life in those who learn from him?

❡ "The first man Adam became a living soul. The last Adam became a life-giving spirit" : what precisely is the nature of that which Christ has bequeathed to mankind through which he becomes genuinely nothing less than a life-giving spirit?

❡ "The sting of death is sin; and the power of sin is the Law" : how obtain freedom from the Law? how acquire conquest over sin? Wherein and whereby does the Lord Jesus Christ contribute to the victory?

§27 STUDIES IN PAUL AS EXPERIENT

℄ "Stablisheth us" : "anointed us" : "sealed us" :
the actor on behalf of these notable outcomes is
represented by Paul as being who?

℄ These outcomes are wrought by the emergence
of what distinctive bestowal? What in man conditions that benign bestowal?

❡ "Ye are an epistle of Christ, written not with ink, but with the Spirit of the living God" : from which it seems evident that the person who becomes truly religious, as Paul understood and taught religion, passes from what state to what status?

❡ "Not of the letter, but of the spirit: for the letter killeth, but the Spirit giveth Life" : since the written code or the Law killeth when taken as the norm to which conduct must be conformed, what alone remains as that possible controlling norm upon the acceptance of which Life through the acquisition of the Spirit is made available?

❡ "The ministration of death". . ."the ministration of condemnation" as over against that of which Paul was the passionate ambassador, namely, "the ministration of the Spirit". . ."the ministration of righteousness" : in view of the vigor and strength of the contrast, what degree of importance attaches to the acquirement of a sound and intelligible understanding of the condition through the fulfilment of which Paul conceived the transition from the one to the other as being achieved?

℘ "Where the Spirit of the Lord is, there is liberty" : liberty from what? liberty without restraint or bounds? liberty with the limits set by some ultimate frame of reference? Liberty to do anything whatsoever that is both immediately and also ultimately for the benefit of whom?

❡ "That the life also of Jesus may be manifested in our body". . ."that the life also of Jesus may be manifested in our mortal flesh" : in order that so supremely impressive an outcome may have its richest possible realization, the condition that must be fulfilled, as set forth here, may be otherwise stated succinctly after what manner?

❧ "Therefore all died". . ."they which live should no longer live unto themselves" : what potential and controllable basic human attitude corresponds in reality to that impressive figure employed here by Paul?

❧ "Wherefore if any man is in Christ, he is a new creature" : in view of the overpowering eminence of the outcome, the profound solicitude is for luminous knowledge of that process through which the outcome is assured : What is that process, that is, how does one become "in Christ"?

⟪ "As having nothing, and yet possessing all things" : in what degree was that notable possession peculiarly the estate of Paul? In what measure is that possession available to those who are willing to learn from Paul?

⟪ "Yet possessing all things" : an extravagant outburst, or simply a sober reality? To be had, if at all, on what terms?

❦ "For your sakes he became poor" : what distinctly personal possession, what alienable area of being, was renounced by Jesus as evidenced by his teaching and by his career?

❦ "That ye through his poverty might become rich" : through what phases of the life of Jesus has humanity been most outstandingly enriched?

ℂ "Bringing every thought into captivity to the obedience of Christ" : what effect upon the clarity, the comprehension, and the convincing conveyance of thought is wrought by absoluteness of obedience?

ℂ How explain the fact that disobedience beclouds the thinking faculty of the disloyal? that the divided will breaks the unity of the mental process?

§35 STUDIES IN PAUL AS EXPERIENT

℘ "His letters, they say, are weighty and strong" :
called upon to fashion descriptive terms covering
the characteristics of the letters of Paul, and to
venture an appraisal as to wherein their most
eminent value consists, what should be the terms
of description and of appraisal?

❡ "The simplicity and the purity that is toward Christ" : in view of the deep solicitude of Paul about the influence of "another Jesus," "a different Spirit," "a different gospel," eagerness is increased on behalf of an understanding as to precisely what Paul covered by "the simplicity and the purity that is toward Christ" : What may one venture to surmise as his intended content for these chosen terms?

ℂ "I speak in foolishness". . ."I speak as one beside himself". . ."If I must needs glory, I will glory of the things that concern my weakness" : (1) what may one learn about the basic condition for sound discipleship to Jesus from the chronicle of events within which these self-estimates stand? (2) what may be deduced as to one outstanding condition or product of loyalty to Jesus from the willingness of Paul soberly to characterize himself by these self-depreciatory terms?

⟪ "But I forbear, lest any man should account of me above that which he seeth me to be, or heareth from me" : since throughout the Letters of Paul he stands loyal to this resolve, never basing his conduct or his teaching upon "visions and revelations," the sources of what he teaches in his Letters must be traced to what several formative and determinative factors which profoundly affected him?

⟪ "When I am weak, then am I strong" : how account intelligibly and adequately for this seemingly strange psychological paradox?

¶ "Jesus Christ is in you" : for that stupendous internal fact to have become an individual reality, what basic condition must inevitably have been fulfilled by the individual?

¶ "Unless indeed ye be reprobate" : what is the ultimate observable evidence as to whether or not the individual is reprobate?

❡ "Every one that believeth" : how fashion an adequate and lucid statement, possessed of convincing power, as to the precise content of what has to be believed in order to the bestowal of salvation?

❡ "A righteousness of God by Faith unto faith" : what is that element in the nature of Faith by virtue of which there resides in its exercise the production of that righteousness which is acceptable to God?

❡ "The righteous shall live by Faith" : studied in its contextual relationship in the Book of Habakkuk (2:4), this quotation contributes what toward the understanding of that Hebrew word which is there translated, in some quarters, by the term "Faith," in other quarters, by the word "faithfulness"?

❡ "The doers of a Law shall be justified" : wherein then consists any necessity for Faith? Or is it to be assumed that this statement is merely hypothetical—there being actually no doers of the Law? Does the alternative, Faith, enable the otherwise impotent to do the Law? Or is the exercise of Faith a mode of escape from the penalty of breaking the Law? Or what is the function of Faith?

❡ "They shew the work of the Law written in their hearts" : so that their problems consist not primarily in knowing what ought to be done, but rather in choosing to do it, and in possessing the power wherewith to conform conduct to the accepted standards : what intelligible contribution does Paul elsewhere make toward the solution of their problems?

℈ "Circumcision is that of the heart, in the spirit, not in the letter" : since the heart is naturally nothing more than another body of flesh, the intelligibility of the saying turns on an understanding of that for which the heart is used as the symbol : what precisely is the reality within man of which the heart is taken as the symbol?

℈ What must happen to that of which the heart is used as the symbol, in order for it to undergo indubitably that process which brings the individual into that intimacy of relationship to God supposedly inherent within the Jewish rite?

⟪ "What if some were without Faith?" : what was the nature of that faith to which reference is made in this observation by Paul?

❡ "The righteousness of God through Faith in Jesus Christ unto all them that believe" : what must one believe, in order that one may be justified freely by the grace of God unto the righteousness of God? How may one come to believe something, thought to be essential to righteousness, which one does not believe and is unable to believe?

℃ "We reckon therefore that a man is justified by Faith apart from the works of the Law" : what does the central term "justified" actually mean? What content should be given to the effective mode covered by the word "Faith"? Whence does one draw the actual norms for specific practical conduct?

℃ "God forbid : nay, we establish the Law" : since Law is declared to be futile as a mode of achieving what is intended by the concept of justification, in what sense can it be affirmed that Law is established?

℄ "Faith was reckoned unto Abraham for right-eousness": Paul founded that sturdy declaration on the statement in Genesis 15:6 : when that affirmation is studied under the influence of its contextual illumination (Genesis 15:1-6), it becomes disclosed that the term "Faith" was interpreted by Paul to mean what?

℄ "Who believe on him that raised Jesus our Lord from the dead" : who was it that raised Jesus from the dead? What does "believe on" God mean, in the light of the historic Abraham episode to which appeal is here made by Paul?

ℭ "Through the Holy Spirit which was given unto us" : upon the fulfilment of what condition does the Spirit of God take possession of the spirit of the individual person?

ℭ What quality of life is regarded here as the attestation of the augmented presence of God within the life of man?

℃ "Christ died for the ungodly". . ."Christ died for us" : whose love was commended toward us by that event—the love of Christ toward us? or the love of God toward us?

℃ What historic evidence is available for support of the position that Jesus consciously chose death with the purpose of thereby commending the love for mankind of somebody—whether his own love for mankind or the love of God for mankind?

℃ "Much more, being reconciled, shall we be saved by his life" : after what manner, or through what process, does the life of Jesus, as contrasted with his death, possess indubitable saving power?

℄ ADAM: "Through one man sin entered into the world, and death through sin". . ."By the trespass of the one the many died". . ."By the trespass of the one, death reigned through the one". . . "Through the one man's disobedience the many were made sinners". . ."Sin reigned in death."

℄ CHRIST: "The grace of God, and the gift by the grace of the one man, Jesus Christ, did abound unto the many". . ."They that receive the abundance of grace and of the gift of righteousness shall reign in life through the one, even Jesus Christ". . ."Grace may reign through righteousness unto eternal life through Jesus Christ our Lord."

℄ BASIS: "Through one act of righteousness the

free gift came unto all men to justification of life". . ."Through the obedience of the one shall the many be made righteous."

℃ CONDITION: Adam was disobedient, and the outcome Death : Christ was obedient, and the outcome Life : To whom was Adam disobedient? to whom was Christ obedient? By what code was Adam confronted? by what code was Christ confronted? For whom the benefits which accrue from Christ—for the disobedient? for the obedient? Obedient or disobedient to what or to whom?

❡ "We who died to sin" : wherein consists essentially the difference between loyal acceptance of and conformity to the Law, on the one hand, and dying to sin as conceived and adopted by Paul as the Way?

❡ "Buried with Christ into death" : since obviously it is not the death of the body that is intended, that which actually must be put to death is what element within the total human personality?

❡ "So we also might walk in newness of life" : an outcome of death to be had through death by the dead person at what stage in the life of the dead person?

❡ "We have become united with him by the likeness of his death" : by whom was that union wrought—by the death of Christ, or by the "death" of the individual?

℃ "Our old man was crucified . . . that so we should no longer be in bondage to sin" : since the outcome is so desirous and so stupendous, utmost lucidity in the apprehension of the process leads to what understanding of the determinative term "crucified"?

℃ "He liveth unto God; even so reckon yourselves alive unto God" : as contrasted with alive unto What or Whom as norm?

❡ "Present yourselves unto God" : wherein does that differ basically from the absolute adoption of the Law as the controlling norm for the guidance of Life and as the way to acceptance by God?

❡ "Sin shall not have dominion over you" : that highly significant state of being is achieved by the abandonment of what and the adoption of what?

§52 STUDIES IN PAUL AS EXPERIENT

❧ "To whom ye present yourselves as servants unto obedience, his servants ye are whom ye obey" : When one chooses to live under the Law, what or whom does one obey? When one chooses to live under Grace, what or whom does one obey? By what process does one pass from living under Law to living under Grace?

❧ "Being made free from sin, and become servants to God, ye have your fruit unto sanctification, and the end eternal life" : what is the difference between being obedient to the Law and becoming servant to God? By what function of the personality does one pass from the one status to the other status?

❡ "Bring forth fruit unto death". . . "Bring forth fruit unto God" : what is the process described here for the passage from the one form of productive outcome to that other which results in Life rather than Death?

❡ "We serve in newness of the Spirit, and not in oldness of the Letter" : whence the derivation of the norms for human conduct under the Spirit when death toward the Letter has been the Way to newness?

℃ "It is no more I that do it, but Sin which dwelleth in me". . ."It is no more I that do it, but Sin which dwelleth in me" : that which is beyond the control of the individual can be brought within the control of the individual only by what happening to the impotent individual?

℃ "To will is present with me, but to do that which is good is not" : where did Paul find what was for him by inheritance an adequate setting forth of that which is good? What could Paul have willed, if anything, that was other than and more than the content of the Law?

℃ "I delight in the Law of God after the inward man: but see a different law in my members, warring against the law of my mind" : what is required from man, if anything, that is other and more than "the inward man" and "my mind" in order that control may emerge naturally and potently over that "different law in my members"?

℃ "The Law is holy, and the commandment holy, and righteous and good". . ."The Law is spiritual" : what does it lack?

℃ "I thank God through Jesus Christ our Lord" : when is the deliverance from the body of this death had by the individual? How does Jesus Christ our Lord effect the deliverance?

℃ " For what the Law could not do, in that it was weak through the flesh, God *effected* . . . . *in order* that the ordinance of the Law might be fulfilled in us, who walk not after the Flesh, but after the Spirit" : by what body of words may one legitimately and lucidly convey the thought of Paul which stands in the text between "God" and "that"—represented above by the succession of seven period marks?

℃ "For the Law of the Spirit of Life in Christ Jesus made me free from the law of sin and of death" : in view of the stupendous outcome, how give content, in lucid terms, as to what is meant by the process, namely, "the Law of the Spirit of Life in Christ Jesus"?

℃ "If any man hath not the Spirit of Christ, he is none of his". . ."The Spirit of him that raised up

Jesus from the dead dwelleth in you" : by the fulfilment of what conditions is this state of being wrought?

℄ "As many as are led by the Spirit of God, these are sons of God" : what does one have to do, in order to be actually led by the Spirit of God? Wherein does that differ from being under the Law?

❡ "Conformed to the image of his Son" : whence may one derive the most dependable knowledge of the basic attitudes and the essential nature of him to whose image one must be conformed?

❡ "Conformed to the image of his Son" : since the individual is declared impotent to conform to what the Law sets as the standard of conduct, wherein consists the justification for the conviction that the individual is competent to conform to "the image of his Son"?

❡ "That he might be the firstborn among many brethren" : what reasonableness resides in the concept of individuals becoming the brethren of one conceived and born after the manner represented in the records about Jesus?

❡ "That he might be the firstborn among many brethren" : what condition for entrance to that brotherhood sharply differentiates it from all other historic or contemporary brotherhoods?

℃ "Present your bodies a living sacrifice" : in view of the strongly and repeatedly asserted efficaciousness of the living sacrifice of the body of Christ, on behalf of mankind, wherein consists the necessity or the potency or the vindication of the act or attitude of an individual here commended by Paul?

℃ "Be ye transformed by the renewing of your mind" : by what lucid terms may one make intelligible that new attitude of mind which results in transformation of character and in profound ethical insight?

℃ "That ye may prove what is the good and acceptable and perfect will of God" : what is the purpose of coming to an understanding of the specific content of the will of God?

❡ "We, who are many, are one body in Christ" : what are the legitimate and intelligible terms by which to convey the basic nature of that bond which constitutes, on the one hand, union with Christ, and, on the other hand, fundamental fellowship with other individuals?

❡ "We are severally members one of another" : under what constraint or norm or directive or agency can that outcome be wrought which indissolubly makes for oneness of an individual with another?

❡ What society on earth presumably is constituted through the acceptance by its individual members of that, and that alone, which conditions the achievement of unity with Christ and with other individuals?

❦ "Thou shalt love thy neighbour as thyself" (Leviticus 19:18) : this injunction directs the individual to find the ethical norms for the control of conduct in relationship to other persons as lodged where? What bearing does this concept of ethical basis have upon the significance and validity of external codes?

❦ "Love worketh no ill to his neighbour" : whether is this fact based in (1) some type of feeling or emotion relative to the neighbour, covered by the word "Love," or in (2) the frame of reference set forth in the determinative words "as thyself"?

❦ "He that loveth his neighbour hath fulfilled the Law". . ."Love therefore is the fulfilment of the Law" : since it is the consistent position of Paul that the natural man cannot keep the ordinances and commandments of the Law because of his inherent impotence, what justification can be offered for presenting and commending some comprehensive general principle covering the Law?

❡ "Have this mind in you, which was also in Christ Jesus" : making the deduction from those qualities set forth by Paul, in this passage, subsequent to this exhortation, by what term or terms should one characterize what Paul conceived to be essentially the mind of Christ?

❡ "Emptied himself, taking the form of a servant" . . ."Humbled himself, becoming obedient even unto death" : in what degree are these attitudes practicable for and obligatory upon the individual who would become a loyal disciple of Jesus?

❡ "Wherefore also God highly exalted him" : what was the essential basis of that exaltation of Jesus by God here asserted by Paul?

⫿ "Have no confidence in the flesh" : judging by the context which follows, what does Paul here mean by "the flesh"?

⫿ "As touching the righteousness which is in the Law, found blameless" : on what dependable basis or understanding may one affirm harmony between this affirmation by Paul about himself and that extended statement concerning his conduct which may be found in §54?

❡ "I count all things to be loss". . ."I suffered the loss of all things" : as the legitimate mode for the effective achievement of some supremely desired outcome, how may this process be otherwise lucidly stated?

❡ "The excellency of the knowledge of Christ Jesus". . ."That I may gain Christ and be found in him" : how may one express, in other terms, the content and meaning of that aspiration which here lures Paul?

❡ "Becoming conformed unto his death" : what may this ideal reasonably be supposed to mean other than and more than bodily death by the mode of crucifixion or otherwise?

❡ "The prize of the high calling of God in Christ Jesus" : to what high calling is one called who would know the high calling of God through the observation of the fundamental attitude of Christ Jesus toward God?

❡ "The circumcision of Christ" : by what two sets of words, within this passage, does Paul adequately cover vividly what he meant by the circumcision of Christ?

❡ "Ye were also raised with Christ". . ."You did God quicken together with Christ" : deriving the statement from these Pauline affirmations of actual outcome, in what terms must the basic function of religion, as experienced and observed by Paul, be finally formulated adequately?

❡ "Ye died" : what content does that concept of what constitutes the effectual religious attitude demand in any use of the prevalent religious central term "Faith"?

❡ "Your life is hid with Christ in God" : by what accepted and chosen process within the individual is that unity with Christ achieved which actuates also as the bond of both with God?

℃ "After the image of him that created him" : in what degree has it been true historically that the function of religion has been obviously conceived and wrought basically as the mode for the contemporary production within society of men like God?

℃ "Christ is all, and in all" : what is that distinctive and basic personal attitude in Christ which, when observed and loyally adopted by the individual, would make within any community of such individuals that basic unity which would become the death of all racial, social, and cultural antagonisms and divisions?

LOCATIONS OF SECTIONS